Book Five

The United States • From Sea to Sea • Moving Forward

Draw · Write · NOW®

by
Marie Hablitzel
and
Kim Stitzer

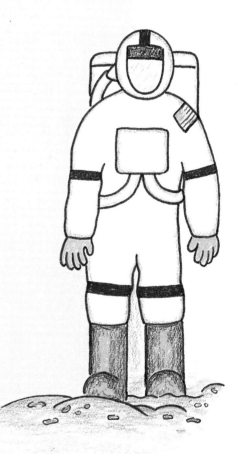

*A Drawing
and Handwriting
Course for Kids!*

Barker Creek Publishing, Inc. • Poulsbo, Washington

Dedicated to…

…my grandchildren.
I have enjoyed drawing with you! — M.H.

…Michelle and Tyler's teachers—Janet L. Kragen, Kristie Freeman and Deb Foreman—K.S.

The authors wish to thank the following for their contributions to this book:
Maureen Todd, Kayte Ruggieri-Vande Putte, Janet L. Kragen and Kurt Brockman.
The authors would also like to thank the following for their professional assistance and encouragement:
Rose Flynn and Virginia Crockett.

The text on the handwriting pages is set in a custom
font created from Marie Hablitzel's handwriting.
The drawings are done using Prismacolor pencils
outlined with a black PaperMate FLAIR!® felt tip pen.

Published by Barker Creek Publishing, Inc.
P.O. Box 2610 • Poulsbo, WA 98370-2610
800•692•5833 FAX: 360•782•2259
www.barkercreek.com

Text and Illustration Copyright © 1998 by Kim Hablitzel Stitzer

Book layout by Judy Richardson
Computer graphics by Jeanne Doran
Printed in USA

Library of Congress Catalog Card Number: 93-73893

Publisher's Cataloging in Publication Data:
Hablitzel, Marie, 1920 - 2007
Draw•Write•Now®, Book Five: A drawing and handwriting course for kids!
(fifth in series)

Summary: A collection of drawing and handwriting lessons for children. *Book Five* focuses on The United States, From Sea to Sea and Moving Forward. Fifth book in the *Draw•Write•Now®* series — 1st ed.

1. Drawing—Technique—Juvenile Literature. 2. Drawing—Study and Teaching (Elementary). 3. Penmanship. 4. United States—History—Juvenile Literature. 5. Presidents—United States—Biography—Juvenile Literature. 6. Inventions—Juvenile Literature. 7. Transportation—Juvenile Literature.
I. Stitzer, Kim, 1956 -   , coauthor. II. Title.
741.2   [372.6]—dc 19

ISBN: 978-0-9639307-5-0

Fifteenth Printing

About this book...

For most children, drawing is their first form of written communication. Long before they master the alphabet and sentence syntax, children express themselves creatively on paper through line and color.

As children mature, their imaginations often race ahead of their drawing skills. By teaching them to see complex objects as combinations of simple shapes and encouraging them to develop their fine-motor skills through regular practice, they can better record the images they see so clearly in their minds.

This book contains a collection of beginning drawing lessons and text for practicing handwriting. These lessons were developed by a teacher who saw her second-grade students becoming increasingly frustrated with their drawing efforts and disenchanted with repetitive handwriting drills.

For more than 30 years, Marie Hablitzel refined what eventually became a daily drawing and handwriting curriculum. Marie's premise was simple—drawing and handwriting require many of the same skills. And, regular practice in a supportive environment is the key to helping children develop their technical skills, self-confidence and creativity.

Coauthors Marie Hablitzel (left) and her daughter, Kim Stitzer

As a classroom teacher, Marie intertwined her daily drawing and handwriting lessons with math, science, social studies, geography, reading and creative writing. She wove an educational tapestry that hundreds of children have found challenging, motivating—and fun!

Although Marie is now retired, her drawing and handwriting lessons continue to be used in the classroom. With the assistance of her daughter, Kim Stitzer, Marie shares more than 150 of her lessons in the eight-volume *Draw•Write•Now*® series.

In *Draw•Write•Now*®, *Book One*, children explore life on a farm, kids and critters and storybook characters. *Books Two* through *Six* feature topics as diverse as Christopher Columbus, the weather, Native Americans, the polar regions, young Abraham Lincoln, beaver ponds and life in the sea. In *Draw•Write•Now*®, *Books Seven* and *Eight*, children circle the globe while learning about animals of the world.

We hope your children and students enjoy these lessons as much as ours have!

—Carolyn Hurst, Publisher

Look for these books in the *Draw•Write•Now*® series...

Book One: On the Farm, Kids and Critters, Storybook Characters
Book Two: Christopher Columbus, Autumn Harvest, The Weather
Book Three: Native Americans, North America, The Pilgrims
Book Four: The Polar Regions, The Arctic, The Antarctic
Book Five: The United States, From Sea to Sea, Moving Forward
Book Six: Animals & Habitats: On Land, Ponds and Rivers, Oceans
Book Seven: Animals of the World, Part I: Forest Animals
Book Eight: Animals of the World, Part II: Grassland and Desert Animals

For additional information call 1-800-692-5833
or visit www.barkercreek.com

Table of Contents

A table of contents is like a map. It guides you to the places you want to visit in a book. Pick a subject you want to draw, then turn to the page listed beside the picture.

For more information on the *Draw•Write•Now®* series, see page 3. For suggestions on how to use this book, see page 6.

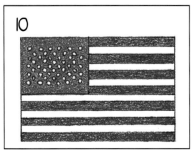
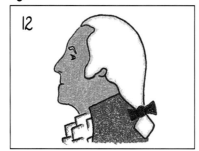
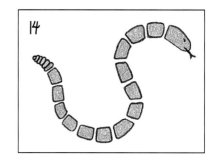

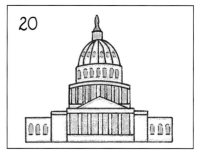
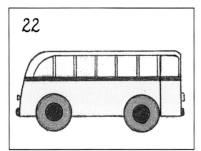 
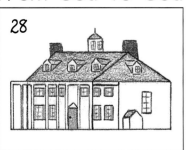
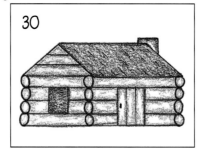

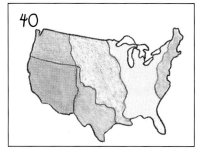
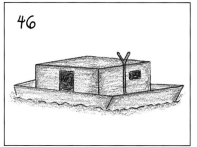

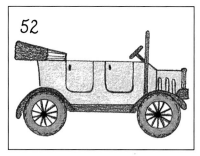
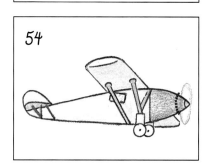
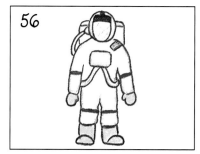
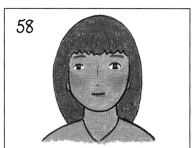

A few tips to get started...

This is a book for children and their parents, teachers and caregivers. Although most young people can complete the lessons in this book quite successfully on their own, a little help and encouragement from a caring adult can go a long way toward building a child's self-confidence, creativity and technical skills.

Alligator by Anna Harrison, age 8
from Draw•Write•Now®, Book Six

The following outline contains insights from the 30-plus years the authors have worked with the material in this book. Realizing that no two children or classrooms are alike, the authors encourage you to modify these lessons to best suit the needs of your child or classroom. Each *Draw•Write•Now®* lesson includes five parts:

    1. Introduce the subject.
    2. Draw the subject.
    3. Draw the background.
    4. Practice handwriting.
    5. Color the drawing.

As presented here, each child will need a pencil, an eraser, drawing paper, penmanship paper and either crayons, color pencils or felt tip markers to complete a lesson.

1. Introduce the Subject
Begin the lesson by generating interest in the subject with a story, discussion, poem, photograph or song. The questions on the illustrated notes scattered throughout this book are examples of how interest can be built along a related theme. Answers to these questions and the titles of several theme-related books are on pages 26, 44 and 62.

2. Draw the Subject
Have the children draw with a pencil. Encourage them to draw lightly because some lines (shown as dashed lines on the drawing lessons) will need to be erased. Show the children the finished drawing in the book. Point out the shapes and lines in the subject as the children work through the lesson. Help the children see that complex objects can be viewed as combinations of lines and simple shapes.

Help the children be successful! Show them how to position the first step on their papers in an appropriate size. Initially, the children may find some shapes difficult to draw. If they do, provide a pattern for them to trace, or draw the first step for them. Once they fine-tune their skills and build their self-confidence, their ability and creativity will take over. For lesson-specific drawing tips and suggestions, refer to *Teaching Tips* on pages 63–64.

3. Draw the Background
Encourage the children to express their creativity and imagination in the backgrounds they add to their pictures. Add to their creative libraries by demonstrating various ways to draw trees, horizons and other details. Point out background details in the drawings in this book, illustrations from other books, photographs and works of art.

Encourage the children to draw their world by looking for basic shapes and lines in the things they see around them. Ask them to draw from their imaginations by using their developing skills. For additional ideas on motivating children to draw creatively, see pages 24–25, 42–43 and 60–61.

4. Practice Handwriting
In place of drills—rows of e's, r's and so on—it is often useful and more motivating to have children write complete sentences when practicing their handwriting. When the focus is on handwriting—rather than spelling or vocabulary enrichment—use simple words that the children can easily read and

spell. Begin by writing each word with the children, demonstrating how individual letters are formed and stressing proper spacing. Start slowly. One or two sentences may be challenging enough in the beginning. Once the children are consistently forming their letters correctly, encourage them to work at their own pace.

There are many ways to adapt these lessons for use with your child or classroom. For example, you may want to replace the authors' text with your own words. You may want to let the children compose sentences to describe their drawings or answer the theme-related questions found throughout the book. You may prefer to replace the block alphabet used in this book with a cursive, D'Nealian® or other alphabet style. If you are unfamiliar with the various alphabet styles used for teaching handwriting, consult your local library. A local elementary school may also be able to recommend an appropriate alphabet style and related resource materials.

5. Color the Picture

Children enjoy coloring their own drawings. The beautiful colors, however, often cover the details they have so carefully drawn in pencil. To preserve their efforts, you may want to have the children trace their pencil lines with black crayons or fine-tipped felt markers.

Crayons—When coloring with crayons, have the children outline their drawings with a black crayon *after* they have colored their pictures (the black crayon may smear if they do their outlining first).

Tepee by Taylor Scott, age 9
from Draw•Write•Now®, Book Three

Deer by Aaron Hagen, age 6
from Draw•Write•Now®, Book Seven

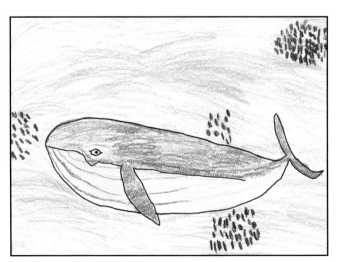

Blue Whale by Joel Brockman, age 7
from Draw•Write•Now®, Book Four

Color Pencils—When coloring with color pencils, have the children outline their drawings with a felt tip marker *before* they color their drawings.

Felt Tip Markers—When coloring with felt tip markers, have the children outline their drawings with a black marker *after* they have colored their pictures.

Your comments are appreciated!
How are you sharing Draw•Write•Now® with your children or students? The authors would appreciate hearing from you. Write to Kim Stitzer, c/o Barker Creek Publishing, P.O. Box 2610, Poulsbo, WA 98370, USA or visit our website at www.barkercreek.com

HANDWRITING IS AN ART

The more you practice, the better your writing will look!

$\mathfrak{We}\ \mathfrak{The}\ \mathfrak{People}$ of the United States in order

Article. 1

Practice Handwriting Carefully

1. Sit up straight.
2. Hold your pencil correctly.
3. Use the paper guidelines.
4. Form each letter carefully.
5. Space the words evenly.
6. Practice daily.

The United States

The Pledge of Allegiance

"I pledge allegiance to the flag of the United States of America"

The flag is a symbol.

It stands for the United States.

The United States has 50 States.

Its flag has 50 stars.

Why do Americans pledge allegiance to a flag?

Flag

Teaching Tip on page 64
Question answered on page 26

The Stars and Stripes

1.

2.

3.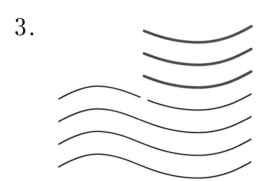

4.

5.

6.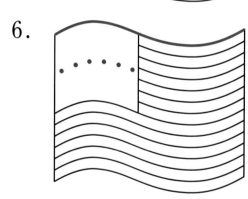

7.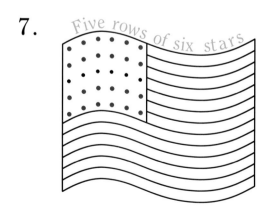

Five rows of six stars

8.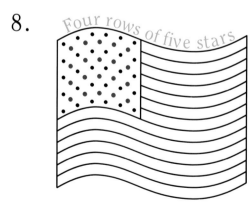

Four rows of five stars

1.

2.

3.

We the People

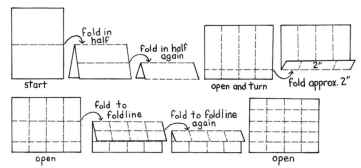

Teaching Tip on page 64
Question answered on page 26

George Washington — First U.S. President

1.

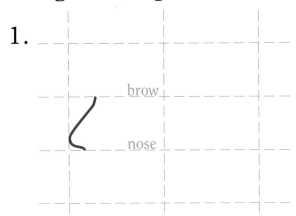

2.

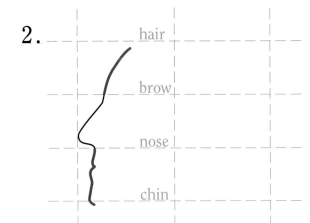

3.

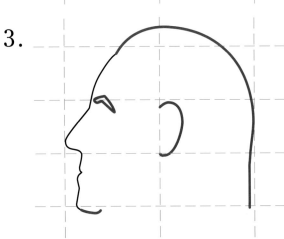

4.

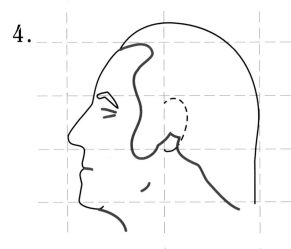

5.

6.

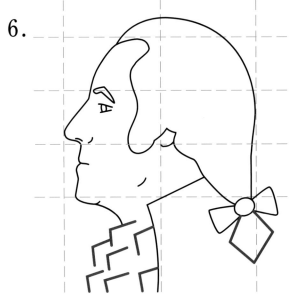

"…and to the republic for which it stands,"

The United States is a republic.
Its leaders work for the people.
The people choose their leaders.
They choose by voting.

Were all Americans able to vote for the first president in 1788?

I Voted

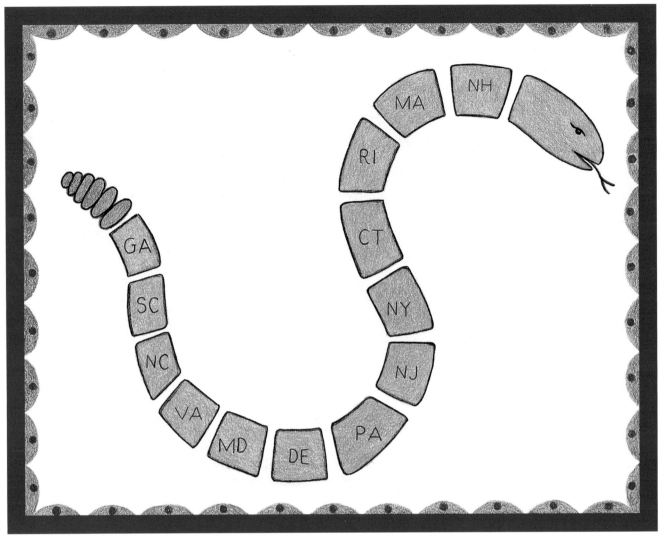

"...one Nation under God,"

There were 13 colonies.

Each was like a small country.

They joined together.

They became the United States.

What did the snake represent?

1776

United We Stand

Question answered on page 26

Don't Tread on Me

1.

2.

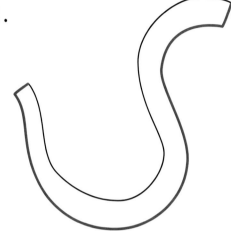

3.

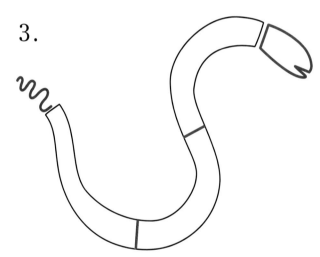

4.

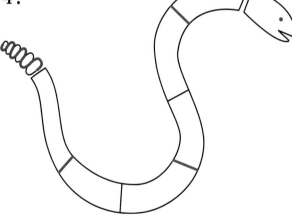

5.

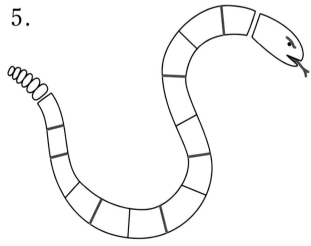

6.

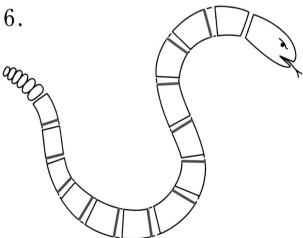

Divided We Fall

Question answered on page 26

Young Abraham Lincoln — Sixteenth U.S. President

1.

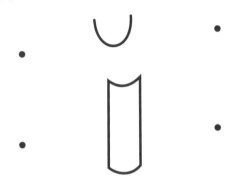

2.

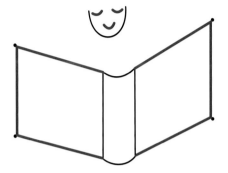

3.

4.

5.

6.

"...indivisible,"

The U.S. began with 13 states.

It grew to 33 states.

Eleven states wanted to leave.

Lincoln said they must stay.

Why do Americans pledge to be indivisible?

"…with liberty"

Americans are proud to be free.
They can make choices.
They can shape their future.
They can voice their ideas.

Liberty

Question answered on page 26

Statue of Liberty

1.

2.

3.

4.

5.

6.

7.

8.

9.

10.

Justice

Question answered on page 26

The Capitol Building — Washington, D.C.

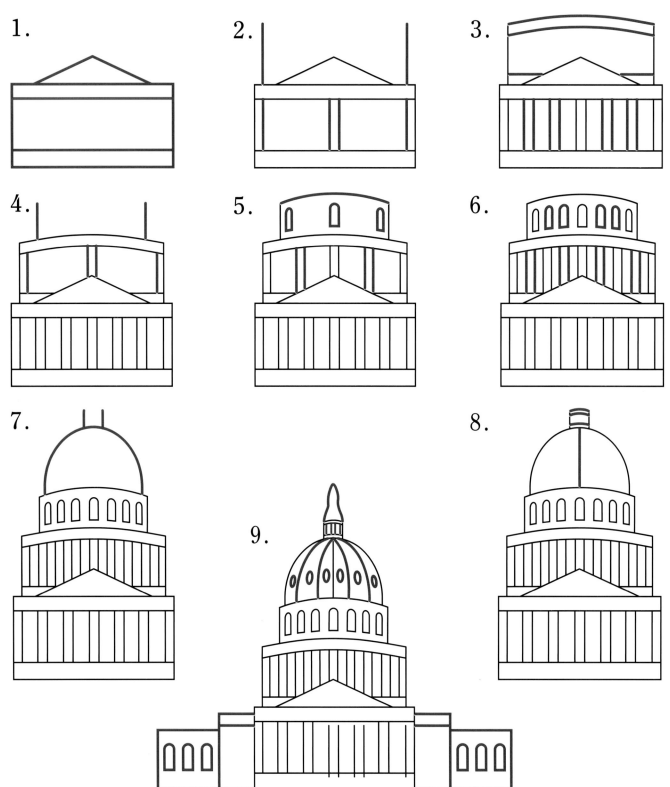

"...and justice"

Justice means being fair.
Americans make their own laws.
They are written by Congress.
Everyone follows the same laws.

What does the word Congress mean?

"...for all."

All Americans are equal.
Each person is important.
One person can make a difference.
One person can help everyone.

How can
one person
help all
Americans?

Rosa Parks

Question answered on page 26

Rosa Parks and the Bus

1.

2.

3.

4.

5.

6.

7.

Draw What You See

Look at American coins...

How have hairstyles
changed through the
years?

1700s

1800s

1900s

How has the symbol for liberty changed
over the years?

Not all coins honor presidents...

Benjamin
Franklin

Susan B.
Anthony

What other Americans may someday have a coin made in their honor?

Dr. Martin
Luther King Jr.

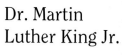

Helen Keller

Draw a coin honoring you!

Learn more about The United States...

WHY DO AMERICANS PLEDGE ALLEGIANCE TO A FLAG? Page 10

To pledge means "to promise". Allegiance means "to love and be true to something." Learn the meaning, history and importance of the pledge in I PLEDGE ALLEGIANCE *by June Swanson, illustrated by Rick Hanson, published by Carolrhoda, 1990.*

WERE ALL AMERICANS ABLE TO VOTE FOR THE FIRST PRESIDENT IN 1788? Page 12

Today, most American citizens over the age of 18 have the right to vote; but in 1788, the only people able to cast a vote for George Washington were white men who owned land. Understand the importance of voting and the frustration of being denied the right to vote with THE BALLOT BOX BATTLE *written and illustrated by Emily Arnold McCully, published by Knopf, 1996. Learn about the first American president in* GEORGE WASHINGTON *by James Cross Giblin, illustrated by Michael Dooling, published by Scholastic, 1992.*

WHAT DID THE SNAKE REPRESENT? Page 14

Before the United States was formed, there were 13 colonies. Each colony operated like a separate country but all were under British rule. Eventually, the colonies wanted to be free from Britian. To succeed, however, the colonies knew they must join together. The snake represented the idea of uniting the 13 colonies to form a new, independent country. The saying, "Don't Tread on Me," demonstrated the respect the colonies demanded. Learn how the United States began with THE FOURTH OF JULY STORY *by Alice Dalgliesh, illustrated by Marie Nonnast, published by Aladdin, 1956.*

WHY DO AMERICANS PLEDGE TO BE INDIVISIBLE? Page 17

The word indivisible means "to stay together". Americans pledge to stay together because the memory of the war between the states is so terrible. Read about the Civil War in THE BLUE AND THE GRAY *by Eve Bunting, illustrated by Ned Bittinger, published by Scholastic, 1996. Learn about Abraham Lincoln, the United States' 16th president, in* HONEST ABE *by Edith Kunhardt, illustrated by Malcah Zeldis, published by Mulberry, 1993 and* LINCOLN: A PHOTOBIOGRAPHY *by Russell Freedman, published by Scholastic, 1987.*

WHAT DOES THE STATUE OF LIBERTY REPRESENT? Page 18

A gift from France, the Statue of Liberty represents the friendship between the countries. It also symbolizes the freedoms — or liberties — people enjoy in America. See COMING TO AMERICA *by Betsy Maestro, illustrated by Susannah Ryan, published by Scholastic, 1996. Also see* THE STORY OF THE STATUE OF LIBERTY *by Betsy and Giulio Maestro, published by Mulberry, 1987.*

WHAT DOES THE WORD CONGRESS MEAN? Page 21

The word congress means "coming together." Learn about the people who formed the United States' first Congress, wrote its Constitution and created The Bill of Rights with A MORE PERFECT UNION *written by Betsy Maestro, illustrated by Giulio Maestro, published by Mulberry, 1987.*

HOW CAN ONE PERSON HELP ALL AMERICANS? Page 22

A single man, woman or child with great conviction can inspire many Americans to work toward positive change. See how one person improved life for many people by challenging unfair state laws in GRANDDADDY'S GIFT *by Margaree King Mitchell, illustrated by Larry Johnson, published by BridgeWater, 1997. Then, flip through an American scrapbook and meet great Americans who inspired others with* MY FELLOW AMERICANS *written and illustrated by Alice Provensen, published by Harcourt Brace, 1995. Rosa Parks inspired the Civil Rights Movement. Hear her story in* I AM ROSA PARKS *by Rosa Parks and Jim Haskins, illustrated by Wil Clay, published by Dial, 1997. For more information on the Civil Rights Movement, read* THE DAY MARTIN LUTHER KING, JR., WAS SHOT *by Jim Haskins, published by Scholastic, 1992.*

E PLURIBUS UNUM

From Sea to Sea

Pacific Ocean

Atlantic Ocean

1776

The U.S. began in the East.
There were large farms.
Many goods were traded.
America traded with Britain.

Did all people live on large farms?

Mount Vernon

1.
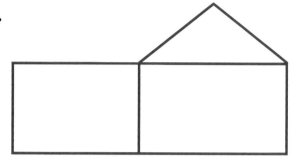

2.
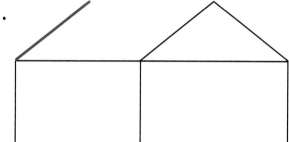

3.
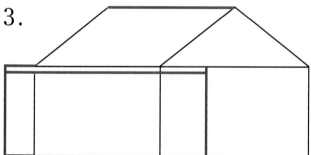

4.
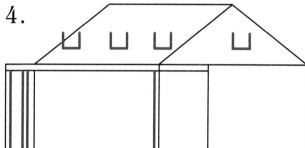

5.
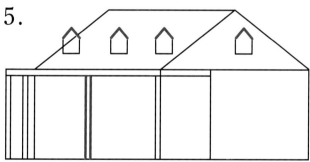

6.
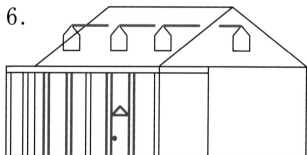

7.
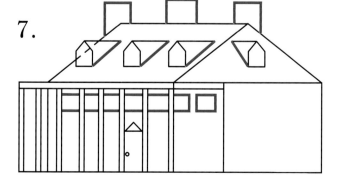

8.

The Frontier

Question answered on page 44

Log Cabin

1.

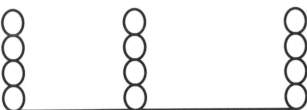

2.

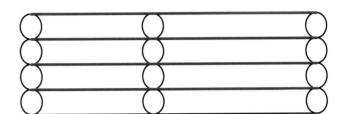

3.

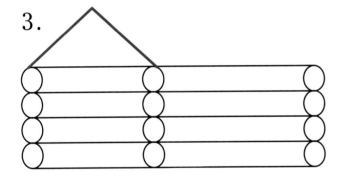

4.

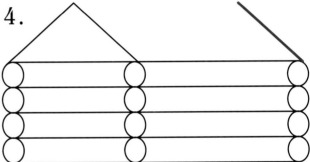

5.

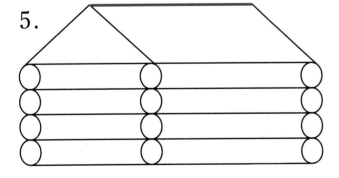

6.

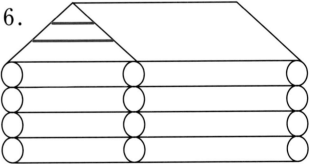

7.

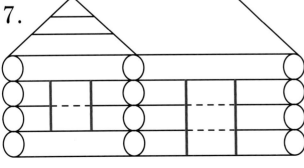

8.

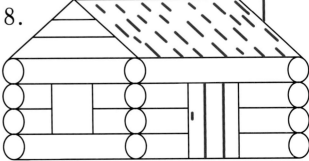

1783

The U.S. gained British land.
It stretched to the Mississippi.
Many people moved west.
They settled the new land.

Why did people want to move west?

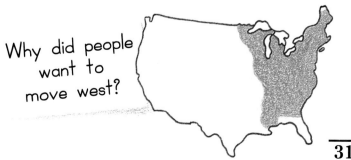

31

1803

France sold land to the U.S.
Little was known about the land.
A group was sent to explore it.
Lewis and Clark led the group.

What did Lewis and Clark hope to find in the new land?

Louisiana Territory

Question answered on page 44

Lewis

1.

2.

3.

4.

5.

Clark

1.

2.

3.

4.

5.

Texas

Teaching Tip on page 64
Question answered on page 44

The Alamo

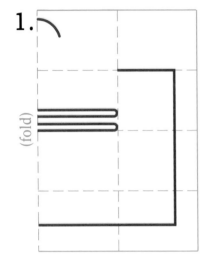

1.

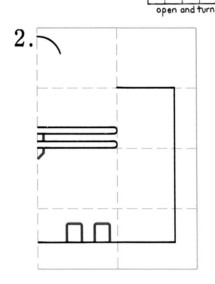

2.

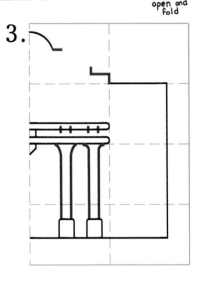

3.

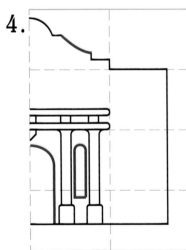

4.

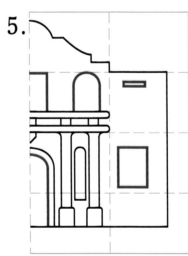

5.

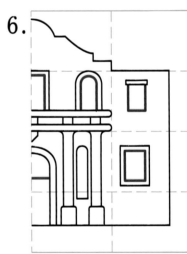

6.

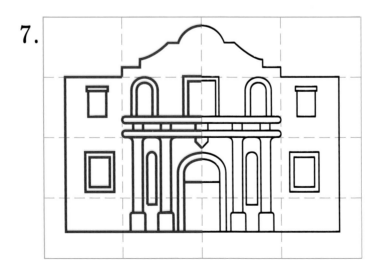

7.

1845

People moved to Texas.
Texas was part of Mexico.
Texans fought for freedom.
Texas joined the U.S.

What lured
Americans
to Texas?

1846

People moved farther west.
Forts were built along the trail.
Britain owned part of the land.
They divided it with the U.S.

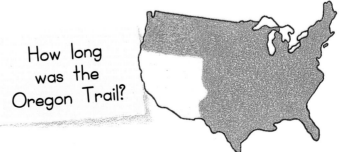

How long was the Oregon Trail?

Oregon Territory

Question answered on page 44

Fort on the Oregon Trail

1.

2.

3.

4.

5.

6.

7.

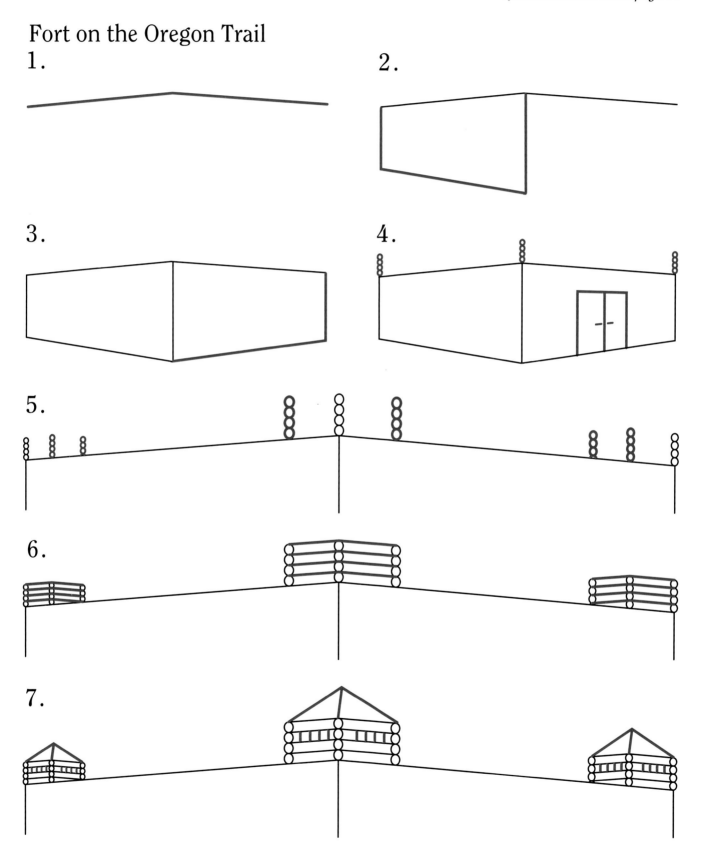

The Southwest

Question answered on page 44

Mining in California

1.

2.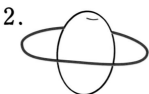

3.

4.

5.

6.

7.

8.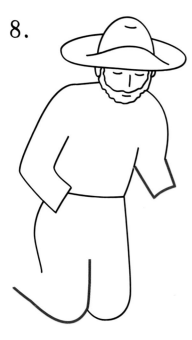

9.

10.

1848

People moved to the Southwest.

It became part of the U.S.

Gold was found in California.

More people rushed west.

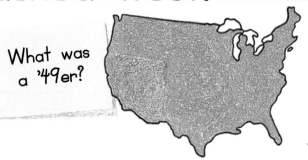

What was a '49er?

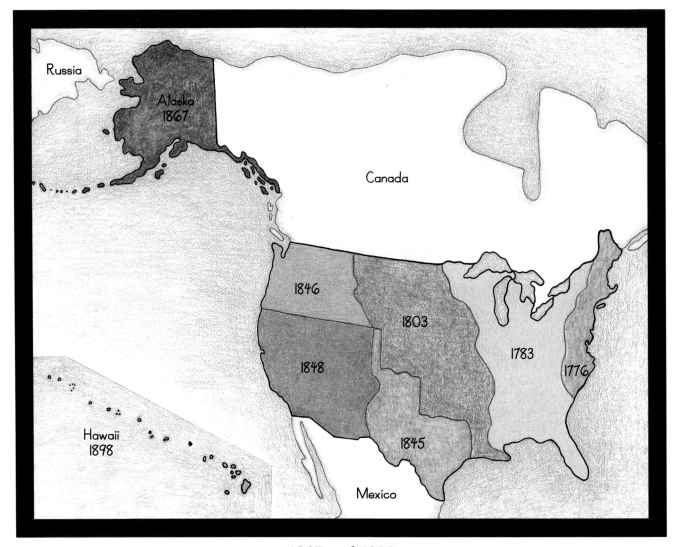

1867 and 1898

Russia sold Alaska to the U.S.

Alaska is north of Canada.

Hawaii joined the U.S. in 1898.

Hawaii is in the Pacific Ocean.

Why did the U.S. add land not connected to its borders?

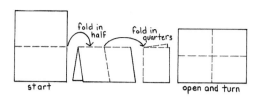

start   fold in half   fold in quarters   open and turn

The Lower 48 States

1.
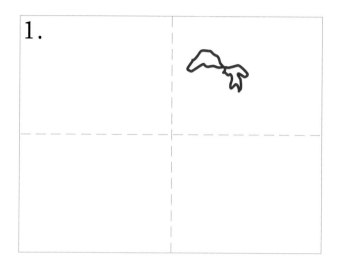

2.
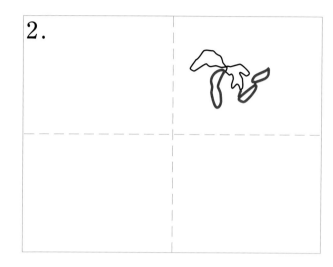

3.
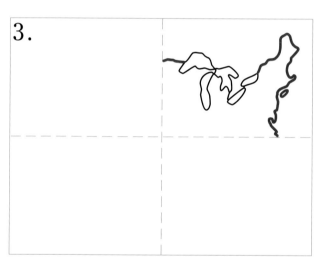

4.
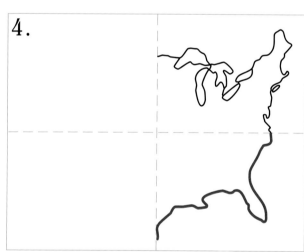

5.
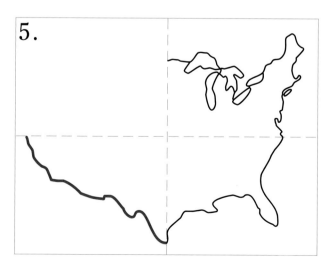

6.
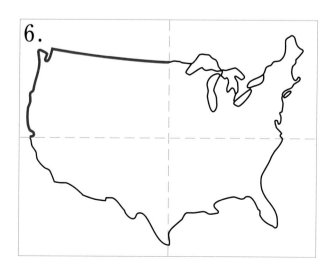

Draw Your World

Do you see the simple shapes used to draw these people?

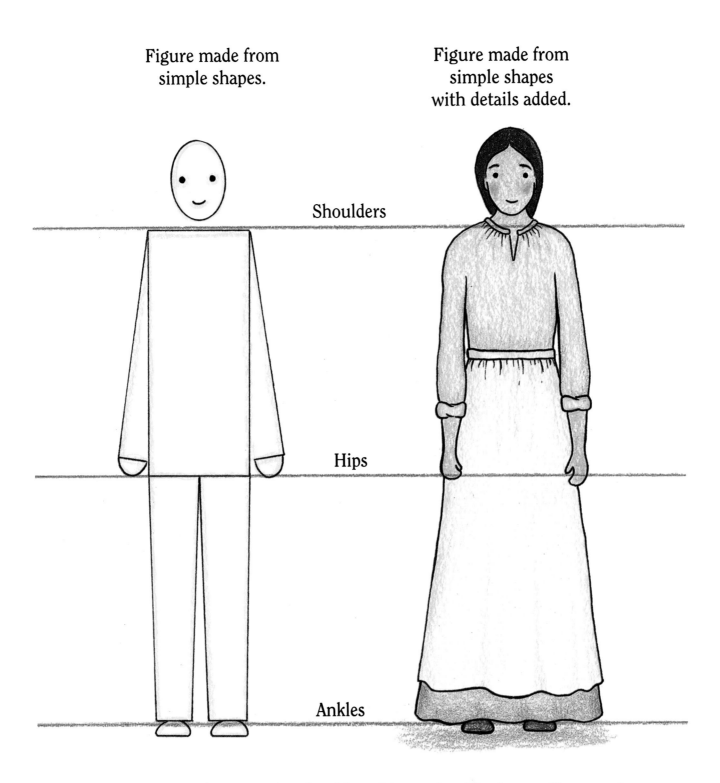

Figure made from simple shapes.

Figure made from simple shapes with details added.

Shoulders

Hips

Ankles

The distance between the shoulders, hips and ankles is equally spaced.

Draw some of the early residents of the United States...

Eskimo

Cowboy

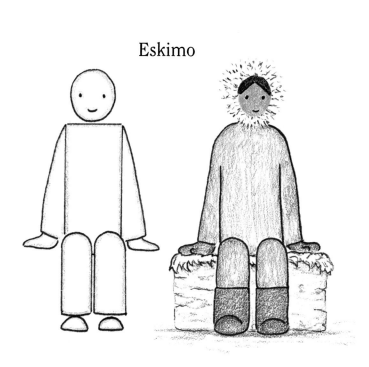

Farmer

Colonial Apprentice

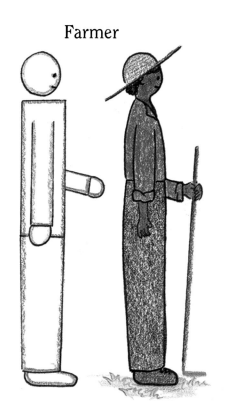

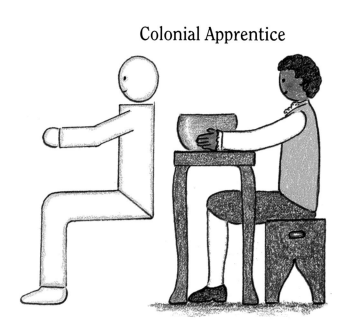

Learn more about the U.S. from sea to sea...

Moving Forward

Long ago, America was different.
Cities were built near water.
People traveled in boats.
Boats carried goods and mail.

What were roads like in the late 1700s?

Flatboat on the Ohio River in 1795

1.

2.

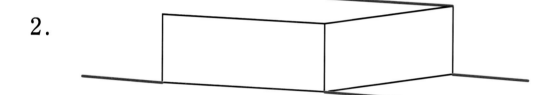

3.

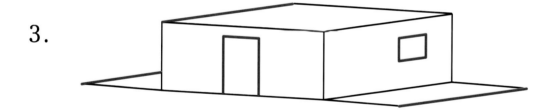

4.

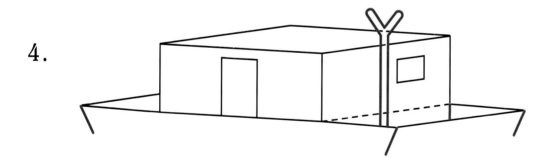

5.

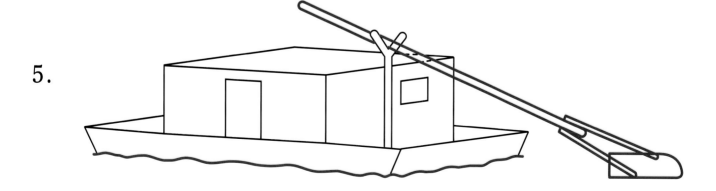

Trails

Question answered on page 44

Covered Wagon on the Oregon Trail in 1850

1.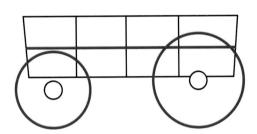

2.

3.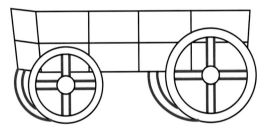

4.

5.

6.

7.

8.

1.

2.

3.

People traveled by land.
They often followed trails.
Many trails were old footpaths.
They were rough and bumpy.

Who made the footpaths that later became wagon trails?

Railroad tracks were laid.
Trains could pull heavy loads.
Railroads linked the country.
Towns grew along the tracks.

How did people send mail before railroads linked the country?

Railroads

Question answered on page 62

Steam Engine on the Transcontinental Railroad in 1869

1.

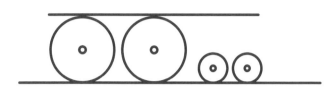

2.

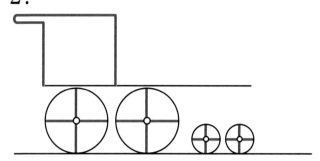

3.

4.

5.

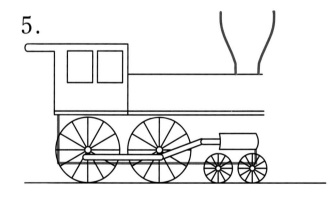

6.

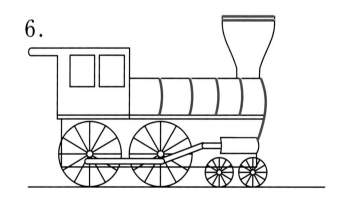

7.

8.

Roadways

Question answered on page 62

Henry Ford's Model T Car in 1908

1.

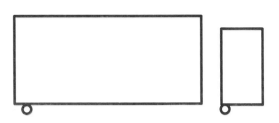

2.

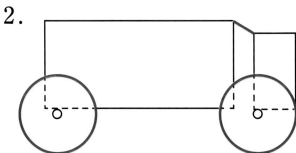

3.

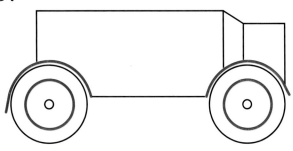

4.

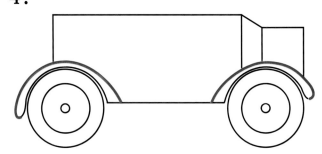

5.

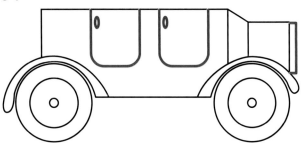

6.

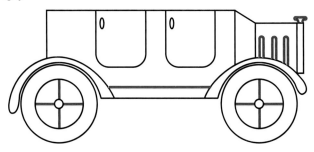

7.

8.

The car was invented.
Early cars were expensive.
Henry Ford built inexpensive cars.
He used an assembly line.

Did other people use Henry Ford's idea?

The first airplane flew in 1903.
The Wright brothers made it.
Early flights were short.
They became longer and longer.

Why did people cheer when The Spirit of St. Louis landed in Paris?

Question answered on page 62

Charles Lindbergh Crossing the Atlantic Ocean in 1927

1.

2.

3.

4.

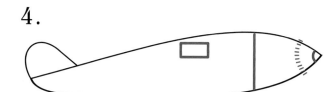

5.

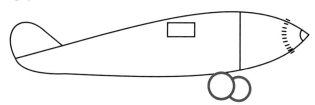

6.

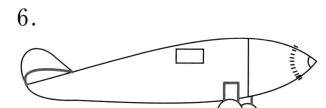

7.

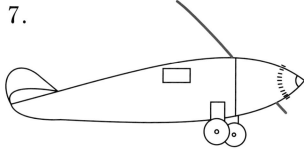

8.

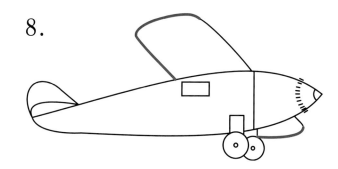

9.

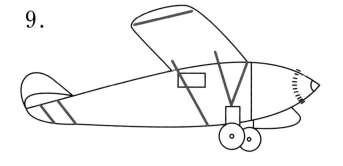

10.

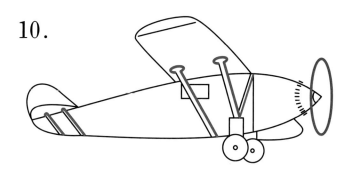

Space Travel

Question answered on page 62

Neil Armstrong Walking on the moon in 1969

1.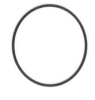

2.

3.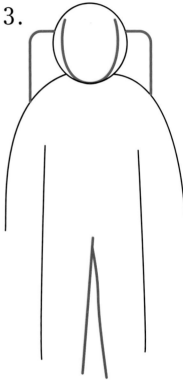

4.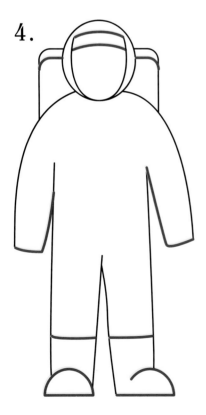

5.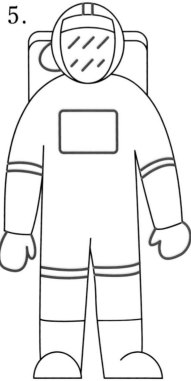

6.

Americans looked to the stars.
They wanted to explore space.
Americans landed on the moon.
People on Earth watched.

How did people watch the astronauts walk on the moon?

Computers do not move.
Yet, computers take us places.
The Internet links computers.
It takes people around the world.

What is the information superhighway?

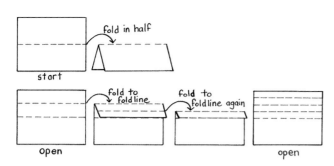

start
fold in half
open
fold to foldline
fold to foldline again
open

Cyberspace

Teaching Tip on page 64
Question answered on page 62

Girl on the Internet in 2000

1.

hair

brow

nose

chin

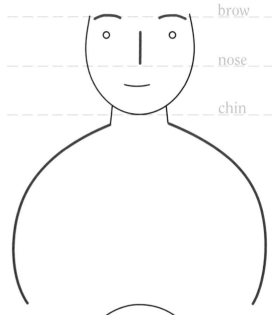

2.

hair

brow

nose

chin

3.

4.

Draw From Your Imagination

How do people move?

Body is straight

Body bends slightly at the waist

Hands bend at the wrists and fingers

Arms bend at the shoulders and elbows

Feet bend down

Body leans back

Legs bend at the hips and knees

Legs and arms are bent

Feet bend at the ankles and toes

Body leans forward

In what direction are these people leaning?

Pony Express Rider
(page 50)

William Clark
(page 32)

Flatboat Navigator
(page 46)

Gold Miner
(page 39)

Thomas Jefferson
(page 8)

Can you stand like these figures?

Learn more about the U.S. Moving Forward...